T5-AFS-762

How to
BUY
or
SELL
a
CAR
by
LONG
DISTANCE

Adams Hudson

Motorbooks International
Publishers & Wholesalers Inc
Osceola, Wisconsin 54020, USA

As with any book of this nature, there must be an adequate disclaimer. An automobile purchase or sale is a legal transaction that can have infinite variations. I have attempted to give reliable and correct information, but I could not cover each and every individual situation regarding transaction legality. Therefore, if you are the least bit unclear of any legal implications, please seek competent legal counsel.

First published in 1987 by Motorbooks International Publishers & Wholesalers Inc, PO Box 2, 729 Prospect Avenue, Osceola, WI 54020 USA

Printed and bound in the United States of America

Motorbooks International books are also available at discounts in bulk quantity for industrial or sales-promotional use. For details write to Special Sales Manager at the Publisher's address

Library of Congress Cataloging-in-Publication Data
Hudson, Adams
    How to buy or sell a car by long distance.

        1. Selling—Automobiles.   2. Automobiles—Purchasing.
3. Advertising—Automobiles.   I. Title.
HF5439.A8H83   1987   629.2'222   87-12185
ISBN 0-87938-259-7 (soft)

Contents

To the guidance of my uncle, Allen
To the understanding of my mother, Katherine
To the patience of my sister, Robin
To the memory of my brother, Tim
To the continual support of my loving wife, Marcia
To the foresight of my publisher
And to the grace of God
Thank you all

Preface

This is a book written purely out of need. Individuals place thousands of automobile ads in national publications each month, but it seems most people don't know what to do next, except perhaps bumble through and hope for the best. I feel the readers of this book can bid those days farewell.

To my knowledge, this is the only book written on this subject. This is an informative guide written with the intent of saving you time, money and headaches. It was never intended to become a coffee-table book. Sure, I considered going four-color, glossy stock with the cover featuring a half-naked girl draped across a Lamborghini, but I didn't feel this was conducive to my message or to the price I'd be forced to charge. I do feel that the information herein will pay for itself.

I encourage you to read both the Buying and Selling sections, regardless of your situation. Looking at the entire picture will enable you to recognize the legitimate concerns of each side, and thus prepare you to deal with them. Obviously, there will be some repetitive information, but I feel this can only serve as positive reinforcement. The Selling section is not a manual on manipulation and the Buying section won't teach you "no money down" techniques. You will soon find that the impetus of any good long-distance purchase involves a great deal of information—reliable, trustworthy information—that flows freely between buyer and seller. I thank you for allowing me to help.

Chapter 1

Buying

So, you've found that car. It's all you could have expected, and then some. Sure, you'll have to attend to some minor details, but aside from that the only other hitch is that it is 810 miles away. What to do next and how to do it best are the major points I am going to cover in this chapter.

People do this all the time and there's nothing to worry about, right? Well, yes to the first part, but there *is* plenty you can do to preclude the worrying, even though most people don't (and they're the ones who worry). Worry and regret are two pretty useless emotions. Some people worry about regrets, and others regret that they ever worried. Each is fairly prevalent in the car-buying market. And if you put some distance between the buyer and the car, you've delved a bit deeper into the unknown, thus increasing the risk. I know I needn't remind you, but you, as the buyer, are assuming most of the risk.

If you have a plan and execute that plan cautiously, you will become and remain way ahead in the transaction. Bartering is a game with no rigid rules or guidelines. Getting a stranger to release information depends on how well your questions are aimed. And not just any information, but the right information. Even the relative interpretation of "excellent" needs to be clarified between two people discussing the same object. There are myriad variables in the area of questions and answers. This is the key to honing in on a good purchase.

I will state here that a good purchase is one in which the buyer and the seller have agreed on all conditions and terms, where neither is to contract unpleasant surprises that weren't a surprise to the other.

Read that again, you know what I mean. Sad but true, the seller sometimes knows about the "surprises," and the buyer is stuck. This situation can lead to the buyer developing a persecution complex of sorts; where he or she feels any and all faults in the car must have been known by the seller. But that's just not so because, first, the seller cannot be expected to know *everything* about the car and, second, the seller is not likely to be psychic about problems yet to arise. The seller is, however, completely accountable for what he states as the truth when the questions are asked. Therefore, again, conducting the interview is crucial.

Preparing for the interview

I fully and completely avow that you can never be overinformed on a purchase of this nature. As previously stated, you, the buyer, are assuming a risky role and you'd best be armed with the munitions of intense research prior to even approaching the bargaining table. The adage "Buyer Beware" applies the instant you decide you are in the market. I hear horror tales of buyer woe daily, and I am most saddened because it usually could have been prevented.

The key is exposure—to magazines, books, car clubs, owners, mechanics and ads that have anything to do with your car. This doesn't mean you need to take a two-year sabbatical and get intimate with Mr. Goodwrench, it only means that a wise purchase can be made in but one way—wisely.

I don't like, in fact I hate, to hear people say something like, "Boy, that Ferrari sure is cute and I've got the money so I'll take it." And thus, unsuspecting buyers leap blindly into the unknown—regarding the car or the seller—and complete a transaction that bears no resemblance to an intelligent purchase. Do they know an engine rebuild will set them back two Yugos? If they had researched it, they would. No sir, I'm not hacking Ferrari one bit, but owning one is entirely different from being attracted to one. It is so with any car.

I know people who have toyed with the idea of purchasing a particular automobile for years, but have never been serious. When they get serious and take the advice on exposure, they suddenly change their entire perspective on the car. Some for the better; some not. In the final analysis, those who follow through escalate their position from casual observer and admirer to qualified purchaser, if not downright authority. They can quote prices from coast to coast; good buys, bad buys, common problems, uncommon options, parts prices, sources, you name it. Now, if you were an unscrupulous seller, would you think this type of person easy prey? Or would you lunge for the uninformed? I thought so. Search, research and shop wisely.

Where, you ask, does a person look to find enough comparables or related information about a particular car? You can begin with magazines to get some good sources, which will in turn give you a wealth of new leads. You have choices of periodicals that range from the 600 pages per month of one-stop-shopping to the finely honed market letters that concentrate on specific automobiles.

If you've yet to be exposed to the automotive book market, you're in for a shock—tens of thousands of titles await you. There are mail order companies that specialize in automotive books; the local library and bookstore are also good sources.

Car clubs advertise in most major auto magazines. I have usually found that the membership dues are offset many times by their usefulness. Most have wonderful magazines or newsletters, local chapters, technical seminars, national meets, club discounts for parts and so on. All share a devotion to their particular marque. In the club roster, you'll probably find people in your area who own your type of automobile. In the newsletter, you'll find mechanics, parts suppliers, maintenance tips and classifieds. All in all, they help immensely in market familiarization, which is what you're after.

If you're not ready to join a car club, or if there's not one for your particular chariot of desire, you need to consult the people who know them best, owners and mechanics. Owners can be contacted by a note on the windshield, classified ads, or through a mechanic who works on the cars. The mechanic can also tell you about any shortcomings or design weaknesses and even give you repair prices.

Concerning car prices, I wanted to save for last the mention of the particular guide books that bankers and insurance companies love to use. When buying a car, they can be quite helpful if used in conjunction with your research knowledge. They are not a substitute, only a supplement. My feeling on this is basically the same as when your English Literature teacher told you to use Cliff's Notes. In her best nasal voice, she said that you can't understand Macbeth in twenty-four minutes. Nor can you assess the market by scanning the guide books. Just because a car is priced at "wholesale" doesn't necessarily make it a good buy. There are plenty of extremes beyond the means, but as is oft said about guide books, they serve as useful reference.

If you are considering buying a truly valuable, supremely rare automobile and can thus justify the expense of an appraiser to give an evaluation, by all means look into it. (I've listed the names of some frequent advertisers for this service in the Appendix.) For your own protection, also seek customer references. There have been cases where appraisers collect a fee from the buyer as well as from the seller to artificially inflate the appraised value. Automobile appraising is, in my opinion, not regulated properly (but then, you will find some dishonesty in nearly every business). Your best bet would be to go with someone with a good, long track record.

Assuming you take some of my advice on market familiarization, you will soon surprise yourself at how quickly your knowledge increases. You may also be surprised at how much fun it is. I know my words sometimes reek of "danger, beware and look out," but that will hopefully maximize your enjoyment. Believe me, I wouldn't have made automobiles a life's study if it hadn't been enjoyable.

The interview

During the initial interview, be straight, clear and concise. Have your questions ready and the ad in front of you. If you just call on a whim and aren't really serious, that's one thing, but if you are a potentially serious buyer, be prepared. You shouldn't make a dozen different calls to the poor guy asking "just one more thing" time and again. I've included a sample inspection outline for questioning (in the Appendix), but there have been too many different types of cars made over the last 100 years for my format to cover them all. The ads will also vary greatly in their completeness. No, that's not a lazy way out for me, but asking how many miles there are on a totally rebuilt 1915 Buick kind of misses the point. Who cares if it's a quarter million, and who would know if it wasn't, and why would it matter on a totally rebuilt car? Don't press the seller on pedantics unless the situation calls for it. This isn't Trivial Pursuit, it is a pursuit of information, and the application of such. Tailoring it to your needs is your department.

A typical conversation may go like this:

"Hello."

"Yes, I'm calling about the car."

"Which car?"

"The one in um . . . the newspaper . . . *Hemmings.*"

"Which one is that?"

"The 1967 E-type coupe."

"Oh, yes, the one in *Road & Track.* And it's a 1965 model."

"Yes, that's it. That's the one."

"Okay, that car is . . . (sold, still available, on fire at the moment and so on)."

This is, I'm afraid, the way a lot of people conduct their initial interview. It's costly and time consuming. And if the seller is a seasoned veteran in ulterior automotives, you'll sound like a good candidate for the drive shaft. Have your questions ready. Have the ad in front of you.

Take two:

"Hello."

"I'm calling about the 1965 E-type coupe in *Road & Track*."

"Yes, I have that."

"If you have a minute, I'd like to ask you a few questions about it, please."

Be polite. Be direct. It's that simple. I can't stand impoliteness. When someone calls and says, "Hey, tell me about your car," I feel like saying, "Hey, tell me about cave life." After all, there is the potential of doing business with each other, so there's no point in acting unbusinesslike or unprofessional, whether this is your profession or not. If you're inquiring about a house, a horse or a houseboat, be direct, be polite.

If the owner *doesn't* have a minute to be quizzed, just leave your name and number, and ask when you can expect his call. This not only means he'll be paying for the return call, but you get to see how well his tentative commitment stacks up. If he says he'll call you in one hour and he calls the next afternoon with no reasonable excuse (if any), you can bet this lax attitude has crept into other areas, like perhaps maintenance of the car in question. And just maybe when he says the brakes were reworked a month or so ago, that could mean he added fluid three months ago.

Every response and reaction has at least a granule of bearing on the whole transaction. Stick to the point of the interview, but also try to establish some degree of familiarity with the seller because the more you get to know the person, the more likely you are to understand his or her reasoning, opinions and motives. Likewise, the less you become "just another caller," the less likely the seller is to leave things undisclosed or tell you an untruth.

Once you're talking with the owner, settle into the one-track-mind mode and ask the questions of greatest importance to you. Again, on the sample outline, the order of questions is a general format I use. Naturally, if the price isn't advertised you'll want to be immediately aware of it. The price, whether you admit it or not, is the single yardstick by which the *overall* condition, rarity and so forth of this car can be measured. "Money is no object" and "A fool and his money . . ." are often interchangeable. I am a firm believer that everyone has their price, however, and any seller who wants you to "just make an offer" is inviting bad relations. Do not, I repeat, do not, make a blind offer. It is expressly the seller's responsibility to place a value unless you are attending a "No reserve, no minimum" auction. In the case of individual car sales, if the seller claims not to know enough about his car (or some other reason) to place a value on it, you may not want to do business with him. There are *extreme* cases where the seller really, truly and honestly doesn't know what something is worth and will just take offers, which is in effect a no reserve auction. This is a very foolish way for the seller to do business, because in any field there are always people qualified to set some value on tangible goods.

Some people prefer to hear all about the car, get a feel for what the price should be, and then ask the price to see if it's higher or lower than their preconception. If it's a lot higher, you'll probably terminate the call and wish you hadn't wasted that money on the phone. If it's a lot lower, you may overreact, and spoil the deal by being too eager, or even end up with a real dog by not looking into why it was so cheap. First, find out the asking price, Poker-face, and if it sounds reasonable, even *very* reasonable, proceed with caution. If the asking price sounds a bit high but still within your means, definitely find out more.

I usually advise people to pay more for nicer examples to avoid future maintenance headaches. If you're a master mechanic or coachworks craftsman, you can take a chance on a car needing repairs. But if you're looking for something to drive and keep, spend a little more to get the better car. Quality endures long after the twinkle of a bargain tarnishes.

Many of you out there are saying something like, "Well, the price isn't in the ad, but I want a 1965 Mustang convertible in red with white only." If the price for a really nice blue with white 1966 model was twenty percent under market value, would you take it? If you *must* have an automatic transmission or other such feature, then this becomes a priority and you needn't compromise at any price. I've found that, oftentimes, people who do settle for something less than what they really wanted will find The Car after they've already committed to another purchase. It's Murphy's second theorem of Buyer Dynamics: The relative likelihood of finding your first-choice purchase increases dramatically *after* the purchase of the second choice. You must decide what is the most important thing to you and inquire about that in the beginning. Then work down through your relative priorities of what could make or break the deal. This is basically a common-sense approach that will save you at least the price of this book in your first few phone calls.

During the interview, stick with a particular subject for as long as you feel is necessary. Let the owner (seller) speak freely, his or her stream of consciousness will work for you. Don't ask a question about the paint, then the tires, then back to the body. Just cover one area at a time so the owner will have the chance to disclose the weak and strong points of that particular area. This will do far more to get the complete picture for both parties. A psychologist friend of mine deems it essential to just "come right out with it" (don't they always?) by using words to the effect: "Certainly no car is perfect, and the more you tell me, good and bad, the better our chances of doing business." Using your own words, let the owner know you're not expecting complete perfection.

Once the owner opens up about a shortcoming or two that doesn't alarm you too terribly, the information flows freely. You are to act as an interviewer, and any good one will tell you that if the interviewee is met with many negative responses, the purpose of interviewing is defeated. In other words, if the owner admits that the exhaust system may need repair, don't shriek, "Oh, my God, the entire system is shot and a stainless replacement will be $600 minimum!" You may certainly say this in your mind, just not with your mouth. Simply inquire as to what parts need repair, or if he's gotten estimates, how good or bad it is and so on, and write it down. The obvious beauty in writing it down means you don't have to have perfect recall when it comes time to "think it through." You can never write down too much.

Any components specified as "rebuilt" should be equally well recorded by you. Definitely ask if the receipts are available, and don't be afraid to ask what the total bill was. Should someone say, for example, that the engine has been rebuilt, you need to find out how extensive the work was. If the owner doesn't have the receipt, ask who did the work and how much it cost. The response may be "I had it rebuilt at Tony's Foreign Car and Saw Sharpening Center" and "Around $175," which means you should talk to Tony about the rebuild first and his shop rates second.

Either way, check it out because these "references" are important since you are screening for quality, or the lack thereof. You have a right to know what you're buying. If the owner doesn't know or remember who did the work, is not sure of the cost, and is sketchy as to when it was done, you're dealing with some of the elements of fabrication. Don't become accusatory, just reiterate what he has told you, "So, we don't know who did the work, how much it cost or when it was done, but it's represented as rebuilt?'' And nothing else. The silence in that pause will either allow the owner to think of a way to prove it, or make him feel guilty, or not let it be represented that way again. In any event, he'll know he's not going to get much by you.

You'll have to judge for yourself what kind of character you're dealing with. The best advice is, if you suspect enough dishonesty to unsettle you but you have no way to prove or disprove it, you should shy away from the deal. There is no tolerance for blatant misrepresentation in a long-distance deal. If it was down the street, you could go get it, check it out, take it to your mechanic, the works. Over long distance, the seller should be able to prove his statements or you'll have to go by what your senses tell you, and if they tell you "No!," listen to them.

Okay, so the car sounds great, the seller has all the receipts, the price is agreeable, and it's not too far away. What next? I'm glad you asked. First, ask for photos—at least three—and get some written confirmation. A copy of the major work receipts wouldn't hurt either, but mainly a general overview of the conversation plus other details is what you're after—in writing.

Sometimes it's not asking too much to choose the photo angles for yourself. The ideal situation would be a front three-quarter, a rear three-quarter (opposite side) and a full shot of the interior. Should the seller be able to send you more, by all means get them. If there are any specific areas of concern for you (an upholstery tear or small dent or something) get a shot of it if you can. On your end of the deal, promise the seller that you will unquestionably return his photos. It doesn't matter how bad they are, how rude he is, or anything else that has nothing to do with the fact that these photos aren't your property. Return them if you're not interested. The seller has obliged in your request and you should return the courtesy. (Idle "photo collectors" bog the system and strip a cooperative person of some valuable advertising tools.)

There are certainly cases where the price is so good that someone who isn't waiting for photos will beat you to the car. Really good buys don't last long, I promise you. Don't think you're the only person out there looking for a $10,000 Pantera. On these occasions, you'll have to direct all your energies into getting enough specific information at the outset so you can decide to travel or not. Making the decision entails judgment, research, feasibility, negotiation and common sense, all equally important.

If all the pieces fall into place concerning the car's condition, options, history, seller's character, location and the like, your next step is to assess the shortcomings and come up with a figure you'd be willing to pay. Sounds simple, but there's more. Assuming you're familiar with the market (and you'd better be), you may have found a car for which the asking price, even with the shortcomings, is right in line. Or the seller may have had little luck in his marketing efforts and be willing to accept offers. If the car is plainly overpriced, make a reasonable offer and leave your name and number. You just may get a call back. (More about this later.) What you'll need to consider is that now, armed with detailed information, photos, documents and so forth, the ball is in your court and you owe the seller some kind of response. If it's just not what you're looking for, send it all back with a brief Thank You note. If it looks promising and you know what you can offer on the car, the next step is to find how you're going to get the car home, and make estimates of those costs, *before* you make the offer.

Travel options

You are now on the threshold of serious consideration. You have four options for getting your driveable car to you: One, fly in, drive home. Two, be driven there, drive home. Three, rent a car one-way, drive home. Four, if you're incredibly fortunate, the seller may bring the car to you. For the nondriveable car, you can only choose to inspect the car first and then you or a transport firm will have to escort the car back. Renting a one-car trailer is not too expensive; paying someone else to do it is.

For the financially elite buying one of Harrah's Bugattis (or similar type), enclosed transport with full payment by bank transfer will suffice. Seriously, if you are looking at an automobile of this caliber and are reading this book, first of all, I'm flattered. Second, you're dealing with a somewhat different set of rules and liabilities, so you should strongly consider hiring an expert. Having a car transported to you is very expensive, and some people do this without ever seeing the car. I do not recommend this approach unless you know the seller very well. End of warning.

Fly in, drive home

This is probably the most common long-distance purchase option. It is also potentially the most costly if you don't buy the car, so I'll issue another caveat: Be as sure about the car as possible before you make the trip. Calculate your expenses each way. Will you be staying in a hotel? Did you get the best rate for airfare—thirty-day advance, super-saver, off-time schedule? How about gas, food, taxi, tolls, car rental? Figure all that's needed for the actual trip in two parts: from home to the car, and from the car back home. Generally, you should deduct only the cost of getting there from the asking price. Assuming you buy the car, getting it home should be your responsibility. If you don't buy the car, you'll need to know the return flight schedule and prices. (Many airline's "advance purchases" carry a penalty if they aren't used, so be thorough.)

Be driven there, drive home

The same rules apply as for the above, but it's occasionally more convenient and almost always less expensive to drive. The ideal situation is to drive with someone who can help with the final decision or a mechanic or someone who thinks like you do, or all three. Also, you'll have another car and driver in case something goes awry.

Taking the bus or train are certainly options, but I've found that the schedules, fares and so on, don't lend themselves to this process, except in unusual situations. These options would be for a drive in the three-hour range, schedules running regularly, not too expensive, with a terminal not too far from the seller. In the years I've done this, no customer has ever chosen these methods, and I have chosen the bus but once. They're great in other circumstances, but not in this particular one.

Rent a car one-way, drive home

This third option is really two options. You can make the entire trip solo (usually for less than air travel) or you can get someone to accompany you and help with the driving. (This is nice for not splitting up the would-be weary travelers.) If you don't buy the car, you just have to rent again to drive home. Of course, the rates for rental cars vary greatly, so check around.

Regarding any of your travel methods, companions and accoutrements need to be chosen carefully. A good friend who is totally unenthused about cars or things mechanical may not remain your friend if forced to help you do an emergency midnight brake job on a 1959 Caddy. Nor would you want to be without tools or a flashlight in this situation. Plan your trip according to what may be needed to get you home. Of course, I've made many trips with only a map and a credit card because this is all the situation really called for. On a final note about travel, it's not highly advisable to take a child on one of these "adventures" if you're the least bit hesitant about the car's mechanical condition. A bad trip could turn them off cars forever, and that really would be a pity.

Making the offer, and negotiations

Warning: If you're serious enough to have gotten

this far, you'll need to be aware of one major consideration before you make any offer: Make certain the car isn't stolen or a rebuilt "totaled" vehicle. (I told you it was major.) In the Appendix are telephone numbers and addresses of title bureaus in their respective states. You'll have to tell them why you're verifying the serial number, and leave a number so they can call you back. Some states require a written request. Failure to do this simple procedure could result in the biggest nightmare imaginable. It happens to people every day, so don't slough it off as something remote. Do it now. Additionally, call the title bureau in your state to find out what's needed to put the car in your name if you do buy it.

You're familiar with the market. You're familiar with the car. You've weighed the travel options and come to terms with the car's value. You're now ready to lay down your cards. The owner doesn't have to take a penny less than his asking price. He doesn't have to allow anything for the condition of the car, the travel, nothing. And depending on how badly you want *this* car, it may not matter. But in most situations, the owner has "padded" his price to allow for a little haggling room. He has advertised in a broad region and should realize that traveling costs will be incurred by someone. If he's not budging on price to accommodate for travel, then he's penalizing those who are farther from him. Have this line of logic firmly planted.

You already know what value you have assigned to the car, and the travel is additional, but it all comes from the same checkbook. Now, if other circumstances happen to take you to the car's location at the right time, consider it fate and go from there. Your total costs for the pursuit and acquisition of the car are what's important.

Your offer needs to contain and reflect all the research you've done. When you make the offer, you'll be able, if need be, to itemize the allowances or comparables in your figure. You may be a little lenient in some of these deductions for the sake of the owner's subsequent "counteroffer," but be fair. If you deduct your air travel based on a first-class, prime-time flight with a couple of Glen Livets, then the owner will correctly figure you for a jerk and maybe call off the deal. At the very least, he'll become harder to deal with. You simply need to be able to give justification for your offer. The fairness, legitimacy and ability to reason with the seller is where a good negotiator makes points. You don't need to go into all the reasons behind your offer unless the seller asks or finds it objectionable.

The seller may be a good arbitrator himself, which will put you in a position of compromising terms or making concessions. Try smoothing the discrepancies before you give in. Example: The seller feels your $500 allowance for tires is exorbitant. You counter by quoting current prices and ask if he has a source that might offer a better deal. Second example: The seller says his mechanic can do such and such for $250 less than what you've been quoted. Tell him you'll gladly adjust your offer if he'll get his mechanic to do the work.

Either way, you're only giving in to reason and sound judgment. The point being that if you sound easy to do business with and are willing to make the deal, you probably will—without overpaying.

Many sellers will hear the first, low offer and make their counteroffer by "splitting the difference." This is an age-old technique equally suited to either side, so anticipate this response. Now you know why making your best offer first isn't usually advisable. If you sense that you're getting close to being accepted, you can often bridge the gap of hesitancy by improving the terms. Tell the owner if he'll accept your offer, you'll mail him a deposit that day. Or that this would be a cash sale. Or that you'll be there with the money the next weekend. Let the owner know that he could consider the car sold, cancel any ads and draw up the papers.

Often, the sheer security and finality of a sincere offer will prompt an owner into acceptance. Whatever the bait, make sure you can stand by your words. If you and the owner remain just too far apart to make the deal, thank him for his time and have him write down your name, number and offer. You'd be surprised how often you'll get called back with an acceptance.

Then again, there are three ways that you may not have to negotiate at all. The first, and most obvious, is a price that's already too good to refuse. It happens. The second is acceptance of your initial offer, in which case, consider yourself fortunate. The last is a technique that works for people who don't go for the haggling game at all. You simply find out what the least acceptable cash offer would be by asking the seller point blank. You'll have to be the judge in considering the negotiations closed or not.

In any event, once you've reached an agreement on price, make your words emphasize commitment. Tell him to consider the car sold at that price and that you'll make immediate arrangements to close the deal.

Your next consideration is time. How long will it be before you can travel to inspect the car and complete the deal? You don't want to travel a great distance just to "look." You want to travel once, prepared to buy if it checks out favorably.

Setting up the closing

At this point, you have settled major concerns without having seen the car. You have answered the who, what, where and how much. You need only decipher when. If you can make the trip soon enough, your words will have to emphasize the utmost intent for consummating the transaction, such as, "Get the paperwork in order, and I'll be there this Friday with a cashier's check." This is a verbal handshake alerting the owner that his part of the bargain is to provide legal, saleable goods and service, for which you are paying the agreed sum.

If for some reason you cannot meet with the owner for a couple of weeks or more, I'm afraid words alone won't cement the deal. Yes, you guessed it—money, in the form of a nonrefundable deposit that will secure the car until your arrival. Two immediate considerations are how much and how long? Naturally, you'll want the answers to be, "not much," and "real long," respectively, but you'll have to use protectionary discretion. If you hesitate at the nonrefundability, you must remember that a refundable deposit may as well be play money because it's really not securing anything. The seller's risk is turning other cash buyers away when you may not even show up. Sure, if you renege he would be entitled to keep the deposit, but he'd much rather follow through with the sale as planned. Fair is fair, so look at it from his side. Your risk is the amount of deposit. The amount varies with the total cost of the car and the length of time it is to secure the car. Usually a deposit will range from a minimum of $100 to $500 or more if the situation calls for it.

A refundable deposit is only applicable in the case where there is not enough available information about a car to solidify your commitment. In this situation, the deposit merely signifies intent, with the understanding that the car might be sold if a cash buyer happens by.

Now, there is the outside chance that the car has been wildly misrepresented and that the person you're dealing with is a real slug. So, for any deposit, send a personal check (it will have long enough to clear the bank before your arrival) with two small imprintings. On the back of the check, type in: The endorsement of this check indicates agreement of all terms, conditions and statements made pertinent to this sale. And on the front, in the blank "For," type: Deposit on (car, serial #).

When you send the deposit, mail it certified, restricted delivery, return receipt. This guarantees delivery directly to the person, with a signed receipt coming back to you. All this will cost you around $3 for anywhere in the United States. That's mighty cheap insurance. With your deposit, send a letter specifying the date, amount, automobile and length of time the deposit shall secure the car. If you know the particulars about your arrival, include them also. Sign it, copy it and mail it. Put the copy and the mail receipt in your file and heave a sigh of relief.

You've just substantially reduced your risk, secured your car and not made the seller feel like an extortionist. And you're thinking, "With all the legalese and such, won't it sound like I don't trust him?" Well, yes it would if you hadn't been doing him a favor. That is, before you sent your deposit, you will have said, "No need to send me a receipt for the deposit, I'll just put it on the check and save you the trouble." And he'll probably thank you.

Every now and then, you'll come across someone who won't deposit the check or gladly refund it if the car is not to your liking. There's a reasonable possibility of dealing with a truly honest, easygoing, no-hurry-to-sell owner who really doesn't want to sell you something you'd be dissatisfied with. That's great. On the other hand, if you find someone trying to pull a fast one and he has any sense at all, he won't cash it either. That's great, too.

An optional safeguard prior to your arrival would be to have a prepurchase inspection performed. This will give you some additional assurance of the car's mechanical fortitude if you're planning to drive it a long way home. You can get the owner's mechanic, someone his mechanic recommends, or go through the yellow pages to find someone qualified to work on this type of automobile. Many mechanics and almost all dealers take credit cards, so you could actually arrange to have the inspection performed, paid for and results given by phone. Of course, you can opt to have it done when you're there if you feel the need. Current costs range from $35 to $150. If you're hesitant about doing your own inspection, this can be money very wisely spent.

Final preparations

In speaking with the owner before your arrival, be absolutely certain about the conditions. Your final checklist should include the following items.

1. A confirmation of price (with or without deposit).

2. How the cashier's check is to be made out—in whose name is the car registered and who is the lienholder?

3. Arrival times translated into the proper time zone (you'd be surprised how often this messes people up).

4. The vehicle's title, tag receipt, bill of sale and other paperwork should be in order ready to be transferred to you.

5. Make sure repair receipts, spare parts and accessories are ready to go with the car. Spare tire good? Tools? Owners manuals?

6. Contact mechanic to confirm prepurchase inspection (optional).

Any items that are considered part of the sale must be at least located before your arrival. You don't want to hear, "Oh yes, the extra set of wheels are definitely in the basement somewhere," only to find out that his wife sold them at a rummage sale two years ago. If there are a bunch of spares with the car, it would be nice to know whether they'll all make the trip back with you or be sent separately. Your passengers will be none too happy if they're forced to make the trip back with a Laycock de Normanville overdrive transmission in their lap.

Should these be too much for the trip back, you'll want some assurance that the items will be sent to you. After all, this is considered a factor in the whole transaction, and you are entitled to them. Sometimes I've been promised immediate delivery on various items that I somehow never received or had to make numerous contacts to get. You can easily make an addendum to the bill of sale that states to the effect, "Any and all items pertinent to this sale shall become the property of (buyer)." It takes about one minute to write this in, and it will protect your interest in whatever spares have been promised.

Dependent upon the length of the trip and the condition of the car, you'll want to pack carefully. Of course, a three- or four-hour jaunt can be done quite easily, but if you are traveling a great distance in a strange or "iffy" automobile, you'll be far better off prepared for the worst. Take a map; use major roads; carry a flashlight, tool bag (if you're handy), roadside flares, adjustable fanbelt, or whatever will make your journey as trauma-free as possible. I know I'm sounding like a paranoid scoutmaster, but it's far better to be overprepared than stranded.

Now, I've covered just about every safeguard except for one triviality—money. This is an area, lest we forget, that the transaction hinges upon. Let's assume you make out the cashier's check for the agreed amount (less deposit, if any), and you fly to Schmucksville only to find a car that's a bit less than was represented. Do you begrudgingly pay full price? Do you pay the man your guaranteed cashier's check and take back his personal check for the amount of the discrepancy? Do you turn around and go home real mad? What will you do, what *will* you do? Well, Karl Malden would be happy to know that I recommend getting cashier's checks for about ninety percent, and traveler's checks for the remainder. This way, you are again protected in the event there are any "misses" (that is, misjudgments, misrepresentations, misunderstandings). You'll still have a convenient means to renegotiate the difference.

You should have the cashier's check made out to the seller *and* yourself so it can't be cashed without *both* signatures. If there is a lien on the car, you'll want it made out to the lienholder also, which requires three signatures to cash. Safe, simple and it costs you nothing, but it could save you the whole amount if it fell into the wrong hands. And, of course, the traveler's checks are equally safe.

You may be thinking that this is a lot of trouble, but look at your options: If you take great wads of cash, you're a fool. If the seller accepts a personal check, he's a fool. If you take only the cashier's check, you're a setup for disappointment. If you take only traveler's checks, well, that's ridiculous. A $10,000 purchase would require 100 $100 checks, and the cost per check would begin to add up. So, in my book (and this is my book), the option of cashier's check plus traveler's checks is The Option.

The last question some of you loopholers may be asking is, "What if there is more than a ten percent discrepancy?" I'll have to answer that with another question. If a person has gotten you to come the distance at your expense and given you information that you feel was less than ninety percent reliable, do you want to do business with him?

Nuts, bolts and brass tacks

Once you've finally viewed the actual car, you'll be able to sort out not only the car's faults but those in the representation. This is where contacting a qualified mechanic for the prepurchase inspection can be important. Now, if the car is just as it was represented, you have a deal. Pay the man his due and proceed. If, however, you've uncovered some "untruths," determining the severity in the difference between what was said and what actually is, will be up to you and your intuition. Most of the time, the owner will have long since recognized your risk in the endeavor and made a fair representation. In addition, he knows he'll ultimately be confronted, which is what a person wanting to get away with something will avoid.

A bold misrepresentation by long distance doesn't happen too often, but it does happen. If things are not at all as you expected, then you should remind the owner of his statements—written and verbal—and point out the discrepancies. There is also your little statement on the back side of the check that bears agreement to those statements. In light of this, ask for a refund because you placed the deposit in good faith on the accuracy of the representation.

I hate to be the harbinger of bad news, but if there's something that just doesn't feel right but bears no blatant error in statement or fact, then you aren't really entitled to a refund.

But that, again, is not a very likely circumstance, which is the good news about the matter. Chances are in your favor that you'll be coming home with a new plaything, and we need to look at how it becomes legally yours.

I've previously made mention of the title bureaus in each state and contend that checking with them will be your safest bet for a hitch-free purchase. There's the chance you'll be buying a car titled in your own state. No problem. Then, there's the chance that checking with the title bureau in another state will hopelessly confuse you and the part-time secretary who should have known better than to answer the phone. When doing your checking, address your questions to the Title Clerk, and be certain you get that person's name. This is so important, I'll say it again: Get the name. It's fine to know *what* you've been told, but if a question should arise, you need to know *who* told you.

The main thing to do when making a legal transfer of ownership is to get the current legal owner to sign the car over to you. This means assigning the title document *and* a bill of sale. (There is a sample bill of sale, in passably proper language, in the Appendix.)

Should the automobile have a lien on it, as in through a bank note, the lienholder will in all likelihood be the titleholder as well. In effect, you'll be buying the car from the bank as well as the owner. Most banks, for example, will hold the title until it is paid all of the amount of the original loan. So, even though a person has paid forty-seven of forty-eight payments, the bank is the titleholder until that last payment is made. Don't get caught between the lender and the borrower. The bank is usually well covered from a legal standpoint and *will* collect—car or money. Now you know why you make the check out to lienholder *and* the owner.

Only in rare circumstances will the actual title be released to an individual who owes money on that car. These cases are when very little money is owed and the banker knows the owner well enough to extend this courtesy, knowing the car is easier to sell with title intact. (It's just plainly less hassle, as you're discovering.) In releasing the title, the lienholder has hopefully stamped "Paid" on the title (now referred to as a clear title, for the obvious reason). If the owner has the title with a lienholder listed, but it is *not* stamped "Paid," well, the title is *not* clear or readily transferable to you. You are then bearing the brunt of another bureaucratic headache.

The status of the title needs to be cleared well in advance of your trip, and in reality is usually less confusing than this paragraph makes it out to be. Determining title status usually requires little more than asking the owner and contacting the title bureau.

Let us continue with the process. I'll assume you have found a trustable owner with a fairly priced car that can be legally and smoothly transferred to you. You are nearing the much-awaited closing. But what about this car you've yet to see . . . will it be worth this anticipatory madness? If you really know cars, you can conduct your own inspection. If you don't know cars and don't care to, you have the prepurchase inspection awaiting you. Should you be somewhere in between or just want some pointers on a casual inspection, you're covered in Chapter 3.

Chapter 2

Selling

Let's take a look at the other lane in this two-way street. You've decided to sell your car and you figure that it is more likely to attract a buyer outside of your local area. If it's a special car, you're exactly right. Certainly the numbers hold true and the expense of national advertising isn't too great when you consider you'll probably get a much higher price for your car. There is the remote chance that your next-door neighbor will buy it, but it just makes good sense to try to market the car to the largest group of potential buyers available.

These buyers are out there. They're just as nutty as we are. And we all appreciate the fact that this would be a mighty dull world if everyone drove Plymouth Valiants. Getting the word out to the buyers is easy enough, but getting the buyers to you is sometimes a problem. They'll call you. They'll talk your ears off asking all sorts of inane questions. They'll get photos of your beloved (not your spouse, your car) and promise they'll be there with a check two weeks from Tuesday. And you never hear from them again.

If this scenario sounds familiar, I commiserate with you. The silver lining is that these jerks prompted the writing of this book, so be thankful. (I knew you would be.) If this is your first time at marketing a car to a broad region, take heed; these pointers are from someone who's been dealing with this for many years.

Each successive year, I'm glad to report, the process has gotten a bit easier. No, the whim-callers, time-wasters and photo-collectors are still out there, multiplying, but with this book, you can make the process flow a little smoother. Mind you that any caller could be The One, so treat each person as such, but be prepared.

Determining value

This is the single most important factor when you decide to sell your car. Even if you're willing to take a trade, you'll need a number to make the trade acceptable. You can consult any of several price guides (see Appendix) for a general idea of what the car is worth. There are also volumes of information contained in the classified ad sections of many automotive magazines (also listed in the Appendix). It is from these ads that you'll see the ad writer's art—or lack thereof—and begin to formulate how your particular car should fare. You may consider calling on a couple of comparable-sounding ads to see if they've sold and for how much. Most owners don't mind telling you if you're polite and tell them your reasons up front. You should only call on ads that are a month or two old, since the chances the car has been sold are greater and the owner's memory is still fresh. If you're having trouble finding *any* comparables, you may have to consult an appraiser or someone who can assess a value for you. (That's right, in the Appendix.) The appraiser will charge a none-too-small fee, but he will give you, in writing, a very valuable sales tool that will represent *your* car in the fairest way possible.

Enhancing the car and yourself

Obviously, there are numerous ways to increase your car's value or saleability. Welcome to the world of improvements. Some improvements may increase the value by less than what they cost you. Some may break even. Others will pay for themselves and then some. All will make the car easier to sell, provided it's a bona fide improvement. Chrome mud flaps and zodiac appliques aren't in this category.

Real improvements can be anything that brings your car up a notch or two in desirability. In this area, you need to think like the buyer would. If ninety-eight percent of cars like yours have cassette players, you can bet it'll serve you well to install one. Or a little freon in the air conditioner to prove its worth, instead of someone thinking the entire system is shot. Other minor maintenance miracles include tune-ups, tire balancing and alignment.

It is these often-overlooked areas that can dramatically increase your car's driveability without spending great wads of money. Consider your evaluation of a car that was hard to start, idled roughly, had poor performance, shook at 55 mph and pulled to the left. If a small expense can offset major negatives, do it. You must simply be considerate of a buyer's first impression.

A complete cleaning and detailing job will do wonders. There is the same psychological reasoning here as not wanting to buy used clothes from an Army/Navy store that need laundering. Even though it's cosmetic attraction in its purest form, an unclean car has a sort of, well, unclean feel to it. You want your car to look and feel proud, which is of course as contagious as laughter. It will also aid in the transference of the car to its new owner if you don't have to hurriedly collect all of your paper clips, loose change and Grand Funk tapes from betwixt the seats. If you don't do another thing to your vehicle before you sell it, get it clean.

Now to the areas that minor repair or cleaning won't rectify: the "needs work" category. If you're selling a car that's worthy of a $2,000 paint job and only have $500, don't paint it. If the leather is cracked and worn, don't cover it with a cheapo vinyl look-alike. Improvements like this aren't improvements at all, they're detriments. If your engine is worn, be prepared to readily disclose it and get a written estimate or two. Be prepared to do the same for any malady. The trust you build will eventually make the sale for you. And you'll sleep better, too. The Golden Rule of Car Selling is, Disclose to others what you would want disclosed to you.

It's a shame that car salespeople are generally perceived as bandits, thieves, liars or otherwise the type who would gleefully cheat Girl Scouts out of change for their cookies. People who sell cars for a living are probably more prone to this perception than those who only do it occasionally. But it trickles down, I promise. If you'll just keep a watchful eye (and tongue) over what is represented and what really *is*, people will appreciate it and that honesty will find its way back to you.

I remember once selling a car that I knew was in below-average condition, and I told the man everything I knew. I pointed out rust spots. I called attention to the slight valve noise. Everything. He bought the car (which was priced accordingly) and later called me to tell me how "pleasant and refreshing it was to deal with someone so straight and honest." I almost cried.

Do what you can to make the sale, but make it honestly. There are plenty of good salespeople—car salespeople included—who are honest. In their customer's opinion, this is why they're so good.

The advertising game

Somewhere in the course of scouring the classifieds, you've probably determined the likely markets for your car. You may have decided that *The Du Pont Registry*, with its four-color glossy photos and lengthy word allowance, is your best bet. But it won't really do if you're selling your rough, but restorable 1966 Corvair. Audiences for different magazines can be as different as are the ballet audience and the pro-wrestling crowd. Each has its likes, attractions and habits that fit that particular magazine, known as demographics. If you majored in advertising, you can put it to use here, but the rest of us just have to get a feel for what crowd which magazines cater to, and go from there. I've compiled a brief synopsis of some major magazines (in the Appendix), but they're *not* the gospel truth. I suggest looking at a copy of any magazine you're considering advertising in to formulate your own opinion.

Computer Listing Services are not my cup of tea

regardless of the hype. They claim to list your automobile for x-dollars until it sells, and they have a couple trillion computer-listed buyers," blah, blah. You may try them at your own risk or talk to someone who has. Good luck.

When you decide where your money is best spent on advertising—be it in two or ten places—hit them simultaneously, or at least during the same period. Your object is to produce the most response from the greatest potential market in the least time. That is, if you really want to sell your car soon. If, for whatever reason, you'd like to draw it out for months, feel free to experiment. My logic is to get the car ready for sale once, promote it like the Olympics, get the response and sell the car. This way, if you tell Mr. Hem McHaw that you have two other people flying in to look at the car, he'll be forced to make a decision and stop wasting both your time and his. The lag time, or time between submitting an ad and its being printed, ranges between one week and maybe three months. So you don't want to be caught deliberating over whether or not to send in an ad because of one person who *might* buy the car. You may want to time your ads for the same print date, or stagger them during the lag period. If you sell the car before a certain ad or ads hit, then you could be entitled to a refund. Even if you're not, just consider it an expense and let it go.

Writing the ad

Somewhere in me is a latent ad copy man. Not that this suppressed persona is any good, mind you, but I do enjoy writing ads. Classified ads are particularly challenging in that the message must be descriptive, alluring, enticing, brief and must relate in the language of your market. ("Brief" is the clincher.) Sounds easy enough, but it's like summarizing a stock speculator as someone who just has to buy low and sell high. As is so often said, Easy rules, but difficult to play well. The best advice I can give you is to read several automotive ads and see what stands out to you. Chances are, they stand out to other people, too. You can learn better by emulation than by trying from scratch. Read as many ads as you can find on your particular car to see what catch phrases occur frequently.

For example, in ads for older Corvettes, you'll often see "numbers match" indicating that the car is an unaltered, unwrecked original. You'll also see "numbers don't match," which is naturally less desirable and priced accordingly, but undeniably up-front. Honesty counts for plenty. BMW owners are fond of putting the factory name for their vehicles' colors in the ad. So, if you don't know "Granatrot" from "Polaris" and are selling a BMW, you'd best find out, because your ad will be speaking to people who do know. There are countless more examples of what language particular car markets respond well to, and reading the ads is the best source material available.

There are perennial favorite phrases to which everyone has a positive response, such as "original owner," "all records," "Enzo Ferrari's personal car." All will do nicely provided you're telling the truth. If you've got low miles, state the amount, not just "low miles," as this is a bit vague. (On the subject of numbers, I don't care if you have four home phone lines and two in your tree house, any more than two phone numbers—presumably work and home—looks like more trouble than it's worth to most callers.)

Now for the number. To price or not to price is a question for many people, and I'm going to take a stand, as you might have guessed. For ninety-eight percent of the cars, put it in the ad. The other two percent would be for the ultra-expensive, exotic or rare models deserving of the adage, If you must ask, you can't afford it. Now, you're thinking of two more exceptions, one being if you're open to offers and the second being if you're trying to lure people into calling you for the sake of finding out the price.

In this order, put the price you'd like to get so the

buyer will have some idea, and follow that with "OBO" (or best offer) or simply "/offers." As for the temptation method, most people won't call just for the price because they usually assume it's too high or you would have included it. Moreover, the ones who do call to find out the price are more likely to be bargain hunters. People looking for "cheap" usually are.

A final word on price inclusion is qualification. When people call long distance on a car whose price is advertised, they've qualified themselves as someone at least looking in your price range.

As far as pricing goes, most everyone "pads" the price somewhat, and I recommend a moderate allowance for haggling. But remember, as the price goes up, the qualified respondents go down, so keep your pad as thin as you and the market can stand.

Preparing for the calls

Before your ads hit, use this anticipatory period to tie up any loose ends. This not only includes readying the car, but also readying you. Round up old receipts for any work done on the car. If you can't find them, call the person who did the work and get a copy. Try to find owners manuals, spare parts, repair books, the original tool kit, touch-up paint; anything that could add that bit of icing that makes your car more attractive. Some of you more fanatical owners already have this taken care of as part of your meticulous routine. Go ahead and pat yourself on the back, because your car will be easier to sell than the average "I think I changed the oil in 1984" guy. You'll almost invariably get a better price, too. Good work.

Also try to anticipate what questions you may be asked, such as: "Oh, you're asking when the tires were put on? Hmmm, well, they've got plenty of tread left." Yeah. Right. You should be prepared: "I bought the tires last July, about 6,500 miles are on them."

When you're assembling the information, you'll want to make a file, however slim, and place everything in it. You should also type up a fact sheet of information about your car and have several copies. You can do it in any form you please as long as it accurately describes your car.

Go ahead and take some glory photos of your car in its most pristine state. Depending on the kind of response you're expecting, you'll want many of the basics: front three-quarter views; rear three-quarter views (other side); interior; and the optional engine, trunk or other particular areas that may need clarification of condition. Get doubles or reprints as necessary.

If you go ahead and do these things before the first call, you'll not have to rush (read botch) the job when the time comes and be waiting for photos to develop while your caller buys another car or loses interest. Speaking of developing, you've doubtless surmised that in all due respect, the insta-print type photos will not do. They must be clear, color photos that show crisp detail.

Keep all of the above in one handy place and you"re on your way to a sale. Somewhere on the fact sheet, make a polite request for the return of your photos if they're not interested. The photos are *your* advertising tools, they're not party favors.

Responding to respondents

When you get your calls, they'll have plenty of questions for you, but you'll definitely want to establish some things for yourself. First, find out where they saw the ad. You've spent money on advertising for one thing: Results. If you should need to renew ads because the car doesn't sell, you'll want to know which ads pulled what responses. It's also just plain good sense to know how well (or poorly) your money was spent.

Second, gauging his interest, get the caller's name, address and phone number. Keep the information and put it in your file. I'll usually make an attempt to get all names and numbers with a brief description of their reaction, which is just a notation for future reference. Should they call you again, you just pull their card and get right back on track with them. They'll be at least mildly flattered.

You'll be able to tell soon enough what kind of caller you have by the line of questioning. You'll hope they give you a chance for a full description before you get into negotiation, but some people like to get the "What will you take?" out of the way first. Either way, listen carefully to them and to yourself during the course of the interview.

Qualifying

There are dozens of ways to "qualify" a buyer, which means to find out what the chances are the sale will go through long before any hopes are built and toppled. Sometimes you can save a lot of time by finding out where the person is calling from to see if closing the deal seems plausible. If you've got a collectible but not too rare a car, it's not likely that someone will travel to Miami from Spokane, Washington, just to see it. Or even half that far. Even if they request photos, simply explain that you appreciate their interest, but you don't think it would be worth the immense effort. If they sound truly sincere after your gentle letdown, go ahead on the outside chance. Acceptable travel distances increase with the exclusivity of the automobile.

On other occasions, you can find out, "Would you be buying the car for yourself?" or "Would this be your first _____?" or "What kind of car would this be replacing?" With any of these questions, you can lead yourself into a wealth of information about the potential buyer. Some of the best responses include, "This is just something I've always wanted, and I have the cash." The bad responses include, "Well, I've got to sell my _____ first." (Be it a DeSoto or a DeLorean, it will take time to sell, so don't hold your breath on this one. Take down the ubiquitous name and number and proceed.) Car salespeople love to ask, "And what business are you in?'' hoping to interpolate your salary versus payments on said vehicle. Not only is this nosey, it has no bearing unless you're planning to finance the car for them. Therefore, their business is the bank's business and none of your business, unless they volunteer it.

A lot of the time, buyers are looking at several cars. They may quote you one that's nicer, closer and priced less than yours. That's fine. If it's so good, let them buy it. If you want to blow them away, *recommend* they buy it. The desired effect here is for you to reduce your price. If you can get them to make an acceptable *offer* on your car, consider it sold, but I usually find that these people are out for the sport and not really serious. Although I've never quite understood it, I'm afraid it all boils down to the fact that some people really have nothing better to do. Woe is them.

The genuinely interested

When you do get interested callers, don't be put off by specific questions that you don't have answers to. If they're of a technical nature, you may want to refer them to your mechanic (be sure to forewarn your mechanic). If they simply ask something you're not readily familiar with, tell them you'll find out. Be sure to include the answer(s) as an addendum to your fact sheet or just call them back. Either way, potential buyers will see you're out to disclose whatever they ask of you, which builds confidence and trust—two very good ingredients for any sale. (More on these subjects later.)

Before you send out your information and photos, you must make a verbal request using language like, ''If the car is really not what you're looking for, would you please return the photos so I may send them to someone else?'' Two things are accomplished: One, you let him know that you're not giving away little tokens of appreciation in photo form; you're serious about selling the car. And, two, you also let him know that the photos *will* be reused and sent to another prospect.

I'm no psychologist, but I feel this registers with a person that if he doesn't buy the car, someone soon will. You'll notice I didn't include the line about "someone else" in the *written* request for photos on the fact sheet. I feel that's a bit presumptuous or an obvious ploy, neither of which is a very smart sales technique. The verbal mention is subtly effective, and if it doesn't work, fine, but it's not a turnoff. The crux of the request is, after all, to simply have your photos returned if they *aren't* going to buy the car.

Once you've mailed the information, it's their turn. They *should* respond shortly thereafter. If after about a week you've not heard back, make a follow-up call. Everyone runs into extenuating circumstances, so let the prospects make their own excuses. After your introduction, say you were checking to make sure they got the information because you hadn't heard anything. This will usually be followed by some excuse, legitimate or otherwise. You be the judge. If they do call you back (or respond favorably to your follow-up call), you've got to concentrate on helping with the decision.

Now, you may have someone who is a seasoned buyer or plain knows what he wants and says, "I'll take it." That being the case, you can proceed to the closing. On other occasions, they'll say they're just not interested. Politely request your photos and put an X by their name in your file. More times than not, however, there will be additional questions, which is understandable. You need to help the prospect through.

Since it would be impossible to handle the infinite combination of reservations, questions or hesitations, I'll stick to the general outline of problem solving. This is for people fairly well on their way to making a commitment, but who are stumbling.

The hesitation point

Take a look at the buyer's side. What specifically is the holdup? How would you feel about it? What would you want done about it? Some people are just very I-don't-know-ish about things until they realize exactly what it is they *do* know and don't like and so on. You'll not only have to help them with defining the problem, but you'll have to devise the solution—no easy task with this type. Question and answer is about the only way to go about it. As you identify the problem, work it through. The number one problem is usually directly or indirectly related to price, but before you organize a Midnight Madness Sale, consider the other "cons," specifically: convenience, consternation and confidence.

Convenience

It's a drive-up window. Or mail order. Or thousands of stores nationwide that make a killing off of convenience. Convenience is really a matter of obstacle removal for the customer. My best negotiating tool in a long-distance sale is one of convenience. It works like a charm and it takes but a small pad out of your price. Before I tell you what it is, again put yourself in the buyer's position. What would be *your* main inconvenience? Travel. That's right. It's an easy answer to an obvious problem. When you suspect travel as the culprit (and it usually is if the distance is more than a two- or three-hour drive), be understanding. Would you be hot-to-trot about spending your good money to fly and look at *his* car?

You need to apply this counteroffer: "I fully understand your situation and the inconvenience, so if you'd like the car, I'll refund your traveling expenses." This offer is usually received positively. Naturally, the refund is contingent upon purchase. Your offer could be used in conjunction with, perhaps, but not instead of: "I'll pick you up at the airport with a full tank of gas." You don't want to use this second line *instead of* because the buyer is worried about getting to you; getting home is *later* and a tank of gas is not much appeasement. In addition, it makes you sound as if you've decided he's going to buy the car without leaving that decision for him to make. You want to lead these people by the hand, not drag them by the ear.

Should prospective serious customers be within the two- or three-hour driving range from you, offer yet a different form of convenience. Tell them you'll be happy to meet them at some halfway point. This will cut their total driving time and mileage in half, and it again shows you're willing to accommodate. People appreciate this.

Depending on the type of customer, you may want to suggest that *if* the car meets their approval (Remember? Leave *his* decision to him), they may want to travel prepared to buy the car and not to have to make a complete second trip. Some people will say that they only want to look and then think about it. That's fine, just be patient and polite. In this instance, you needn't have anyone follow you to the halfway point. On the other hand, some will respond that they will be traveling prepared to purchase. Make sure they bring cash or a cashier's check and you make sure to have someone follow you. I've done numerous closings at Interstate rest areas. You will need to arrive with the necessary paperwork to sell the car. (The standard items and the optional equipment are discussed elsewhere.) Obviously, the more prepared you are, the greater the chances of making the sale.

This is the point of convenience selling. Anything you can think of that would or could possibly facilitate the sale—Do It. A cassette tape to show the cassette player works. A clean rag to wipe a curious hand. A pen that writes. An old blanket for looking under the car. You name it. Any item conducive to the inspection, road test or the actual sale is something you do not want to be without. Modern man is a creature geared for the delight of convenience. Don't you forget it.

Consternation

Webster defines it as "Amazement or dismay that hinders or throws one into a state of confusion." This is precisely what happens to the first-time long-distance buyer. As a broker of autos across the land, my number one question from someone ready to buy is: "Now what do I do?" Think about it. These people have checked into the car. They have weighed the entire situation, made a decision to pursue, agreed on a price and have the money. And the question is, for those of you who may have missed it, "Now what do I do?" It is partly for that single question that I decided to write this book. It is also why I take the stand now, as in the Preface, to recommend that you read the *Buying* section of this book. In the interest of understanding both sides, I feel you can only benefit from reading The Rest of the Story.

Naturally, there *are* people who are incapable of making up their minds on the car and not the process, at least for now. You'll have to assume the sounding board role here and ask a few point-blank questions: "Is there anything you're unclear or unsure of that I can help you with? Would it be helpful if I gave you a night to think it over? Would it help if I sent you a picture of the _____? Or got an estimate? Or a compression check? Or have your mechanic call mine?" Be creative if you must, but ASK or you'll never decipher the problem. Remember, we're not discussing problems with price, we're dealing with pure, unadulterated indecisiveness. Many of us are hesitant about a purchase for numerous reasons that have nothing to do with price. You need to identify the reservations of your prospect and come to a solution. This, coupled with your obvious willingness to cooperate, will bring us smoothly into the next area.

Confidence

All you've done up to this point should certainly

inspire if not exude confidence. He asks. You tell. You don't know. You find out. Good, bad or indifferent. This is simply a matter of understanding. As more trust and open communication flows between you, confidence builds. This eventually erases the need for any high-powered techniques of the mega-salesperson. Confidence is not earned by trickery or manipulation. Confidence either will or will not be built by you. Your actions and reactions will govern the barometer of confidence. It is a very natural by-product of open, honest, responsible interaction. You'll lose sale after sale without it. Yes, some things do sell themselves. And mostly, those things are new and able to be readily inspected, or are the object of "frenzy buying," none of which we're dealing with here. Your car is very likely to remain unsold unless you can get someone to look at it. A buyer will need to have confidence in you and your word to make the trip.

Salesmanship

This is an area that, while composing this book, I had feared to tread. But the time is right, so here goes.

The basics of selling have remained unchanged since Og sold Ug his first rock. The times have dictated myriad technical and communicative enhancements, but the rules remain the same. I have learned from and listened to many salespeople—good and bad. From past experience, I have seen myself as both, and you *learn* just as much from realizing what *not* to do in making a sale. But that puts you into the process of elimination, and we all know that it's easier to be taught the right way first. Ineffective selling is therefore not without a bit of redemption. However, effective positive selling is the goal.

Since I didn't and still don't intend for this to be a "How to Sell, Sell, Sell" type of book, I'll be brief. In fact, I'll limit you patient readers to three major areas of selling basics.

1. *Each inquirer about your car is a customer*. The wide-eyed youth who asks how fast it will go or the grandmother who asks what it is. They are your customers. The man without a penny who asks how much it costs is your customer. No impoliteness. No rudeness. No "No time for you"-ness.

In a way, we all know each other somehow. If you know her and she knows them, then they all know you . . . in that way. When you've remarked, "Small world," wasn't it usually the case that you had an entirely unlikely link with a chain of acquaintances? Same thing. Everybody knows somebody you don't. Should you mistreat a customer—that is, *anybody* as in the previous paragraph—you can bet they aren't friends with anybody who's going to buy from you. Very simple. It's the boomerang effect, and I am a firm believer in it. For each person you are in pleasant contact with, you're indirectly in contact with a hundred-fold others.

It's a rather negative reflection on society, but people have a tendency to repeat a story of mistreatment more often than one that went along with no hitches. Why? Because a story with no hitches is a dull story. When was the last time you heard someone volunteer, "Well, I went to buy this car, and the guy sold it to me, and I'm happy." Gee, then what happened? Big deal. Now think about the dozens of "That SOB who sold me this . . ." type stories you've heard. Get the picture? Each inquirer is your customer.

2. *Talk silently to your ears while you watch your mouth*. This simply requires, in sequence: effective listening, interpretation and application (or reaction) of what you've heard. You must listen to your customer. His needs. His wishes. His limitations. Tailor the language of your representation so he can understand and relate to it. You can tell a mechanic that the A-arm bushing has worn and de-cambered the front end geometry, but you tell a novice that the front

wheels need alignment work. Same message, different language.

On this basic sales rule, just remember to think. To actively take a personal stake in what your customer needs. And you *do* have a personal stake in it. After all, it's your car you're trying to sell. But if it's not right for him, don't push it. There will be other customers, and who knows, this one just may call you back and tell you he'll take it. Or maybe he knows someone who will. Stranger things have happened.

If you ever go through one of your "sales pitches" and realize that you sound pushy, you've gone too far. In sales, wordiness is next to pushiness. Not one person on the planet Earth likes a pushy salesperson. Talk silently to your ears while you watch your mouth.

3. *Each missed sale puts you closer to your goal.* Paradoxical indeed. Don't get discouraged when you don't make the sale, because the law of averages says each prospect is more likely to buy than the one before who didn't. If you've done all you can to make the sale and it doesn't go through, forget it and move on. Be sure to meet the next prospect fresh, armed with the new knowledge gathered from the last, but with none of the defeated attitude. The only things that are to be carried over from a missed sale are the fruit-bearing seeds of knowledge. Not remorse. Not regret. People buy from winners and shy away from losers. You cannot adopt a "woe-is-me" attitude when you realize this truth. Each missed sale puts you closer to your goal.

There are hundreds of motivational books, recordings and seminars on selling, and any one may be worth a try if you're that involved. I believe the above three points cover enough territory to keep the passably interested salesperson in check, but if it has only whet your appetite for more, please consult your local library or bookseller. Tell them Ug sent you.

Receiving offers/negotiations

At this point, you will come to grips with the all-important "number." Should you really have a firm price, hold to it. You may just be "feeling the market" to see what kinds of buyers and prices are out there. I've done that myself. However, I'll assume you are serious about selling, since you've bought this book and have read thus far. So when an offer comes, you must know how to accept or decline, and negotiate back into acceptance. Negotiations may possibly never enter the picture, which can only mean the best—that the offer is good and the car is sold. But usually there's more to it.

When I discussed the convenience aspect of selling, I touched on an effective negotiating tool, and as you doubtless noticed, you had to essentially compromise your asking price. This is what negotiations are all about. Allow me to introduce you to negotiating:

"Conditions, meet Conflict."

"Conflict, meet Compromise."

"Hello, Solution."

This is a simplistic but very real version of negotiating into acceptance. I only wish it were so simple. We'll take a look at the profile so you can get a better understanding of striking a deal.

You have a tug-of-war based on bipolar differences. The buyer wants to spend as little as possible. The seller wants to get as much as possible. But you both basically want the deal to go through. There is a solution somewhere. You, the seller, *know* the price you need to get, the buyer doesn't. If you need to get more than the car is worth, you've got a tough road ahead of you. This is why value determination is extremely important. Price it too high and you turn people off. Price it too low and you lose money.

We should look at a hypothetical situation where you, the seller, are not in the most enviable position. Obviously, if your first offer is acceptable and you don't feel like milking the customer for a couple hundred dollars (and risk losing him), you accept. We want to look at the situation of having had few, if any, calls on the car. The ad's "shelf life" is running low, and you've yet to get an offer, until now. That's the situation, here's how to proceed.

Let's assume that a buyer, based on your fair, accurate description, has made an offer. Not necessarily a "lowball" offer (one so low that if even half of what you said was true, he couldn't lose. Dealers often do this to protect their high-risk position). We'll say he has offered $8,500 on a car you priced at $10,000. That's a pretty big whack off your price, but you will accept between $9,200 and $9,400 net. Now let's make some assumptions about his offer:

1. His offer is based on him paying his own travel expenses.

2. He is very much interested in your car to have made an offer at all. He is eighty-five percent up to your *asking* price, which is looking at the bright side, even though you must bridge roughly a $1,000 gap.

3. He has not made his highest offer first. He needs reassurance that he can safely allow himself to up his offer into an acceptable one.

4. Something has registered as a negative in his mind regarding your asking price. (a) The asking price was simply too high for this type car, regardless of condition. Or (b) the condition of this type car is not reflective of its asking price. Or (c) he is the type who knows your price is padded to a degree and would have made an offer lower than *any* asking price. (Related to No. 3.)

You need to respond to his offer by first surmising which reason(s) caused him to reduce your asking price by nearly twenty percent. Start with convenience selling, if he was basing his offer on having to pay for the trip, and work through his "cons" as discussed earlier. For example, if the plane fare should run $250, you're covered on any offer that allows you $250 or more over your least acceptable price.

He may haggle his way up to $9,000 and be willing to pay his own way. This is a good position for you because the halfway point between his offer and your price is acceptable to you. Therefore, tell him you'll split the difference with him, and he's got a car. In other words, if he'll go half way, you'll go half way, or $9,500. Bingo. But never offer to split the difference if that number is unacceptable. You can't expect to "bump" someone more than once. You could even forego this and split the difference between his original $8,500 offer and the $10,000 (that is, $9,250), which is acceptable, but dangerously low, especially if he balks.

Should you have trouble moving the customer at all, you'll need another approach. Again, you must be at first appreciative of his offer. Or even apologetic that you can't accept it. Believe me, the last thing you need to do is make him feel cheap. (Even though he may be, but in this hypothetical example, he is your only serious nibble.) Here's how it might go:

Seller: "I do wish I could take your offer, but we're not too far apart in price. Maybe we can work something out."

Buyer: "Well, I'm not interested in paying any more than $8,500 for the car."

Seller: "Have you checked out other cars in this condition and at this price?" (You have, remember?)

Buyer: "Well, I've called on a few that sounded close."

Seller: "What was the verdict? Had they sold or were they not right somehow?"

Okay, here you have asked him for comparables, to see if other cars like yours are selling for or near $8,500. You're looking for fact, not emotion. And your last question is a "probe." What does the current market status (from his observation) prove? You've given him the opportunity to quote you reasons he didn't buy the other cars. Listen to this carefully and interpret every syllable. If any of the other cars have sold, you need to find out their price and gear your response: "The one that sold for less than mine probably just plainly wasn't worth as much because . . ." Name and reiterate your car's best, most unique features.

If the car was as good as yours, was it a fluke? Find out. Get the phone number and call to find out. Ask the former owner if he has any names or numbers of those who didn't buy his car. Where did he advertise? What was his car really like? Give him your name and number for anybody else who may call on his ad so he can refer them. Congratulate him on having sold his car, and thank him very much for his help.

Back to your buyer and his response that he *hasn't* checked on any others. Here you've got someone who probably doesn't know a good deal when he sees one, so meet him head on, again with facts of your own.

Seller: "Well, I've got an appraisal for $10,000" or "I see four others advertised in excess of $10,000" or "My guide book quotes prices for cars in my condition at _____." Then go over the best features of your car and compound your efforts with convenience offers. And perhaps, use a battery of enticements: "Okay, I see two others advertised at $10,500, one for $10,800, and another for $11,200." (No need in quoting cars priced lower unless their ad indicated a condition far beneath yours.) "I'll offer the car to you for $9,800 *and* pay for your airfare. Does that sound acceptable to you?"

This should be hard for him to resist. Any of these negotiating tools can be used independently or in conjunction with others, but use your head and never, never accept one penny less than you'll regret.

You may have a car that will sell on the first day the ad comes out. Then again, your car may remain on the market for months. Depending on your eagerness to sell, your price may have to be lowered in subsequent advertising. If you do this, be sure to change the entire verbiage of the ad, along with the price. Should you leave your ad the same, but change only the price, you put three negatives against yourself: First, people who are familiar with the original ad and price will assume you're having a difficult time selling your car because something is wrong with it. Second, people who regularly read the ads will scan over yours not even noticing the price change because they assume they've already seen your ad. And third, you're still paying for this ad and have excluded two big groups of ad readers.

I must share a classic example of this with you. I remember reading a series of similar ads in various publications that touted the auto for sale as "ex-Pete Rose car." The fact that ol' Pete had owned it probably added to the value for some people, but as nice as the car sounded, it was still overpriced. Over the next *several* months, I continued to see the Pete Rose car for sale, albeit the price was dropping. It seems the car was *still* being offered over a year after it first appeared with the same wording at what became a real bargain of a price. I never called on the car. Why? Well, just as I told you, I thought the car must have been a smoldering wreck or that Pete had used it for a backstop or something and nobody wanted it. I'm definitely not saying my assumption was accurate, because the rest of the ad said it was a good car, and it may well have been a great car. I'm merely illustrating a point that cars which are to be re-advertised should use a change-up pitch. (Sorry, I couldn't resist it.)

At some point during your efforts, you will get an acceptable offer. We shall discuss next how to arrange and ultimately close the deal.

Setting up the closing

Okay, someone is enamored enough with your car to make an acceptable offer. That's fabulous. You should at first be very glad for yourself, but don't quite kick back and relax just yet. The hard part is basically done, provided the buyer is not in for any surprises about your car, the tentative agreement is at least fifty percent set. That agreement being: If your car is what you say (and of course it is), he will pay what he has offered. So far so good, but that second fifty percent needs some assurance. What you each need now is security to bond this verbal contract. If the buyer can come to look at the car and close the deal readily, get him to make his plans and tell you exactly when that is to be. More often, there will be a couple or three weeks before mutual schedules allow for a meeting, so you'll need additional security in the form of a nonrefundable deposit.

A deposit is "earnest money." It binds the bargain. It shows intent. The deposit will hold the car until the buyer's arrival. It is essential when there is a delay, so you are able to consider the car sold. Should the buyer make his offer but be hesitant about the deposit, simply remind him that the deposit is to ensure *his* security in the matter as well. That is, if someone comes up to you with cash in hand and you've already taken a deposit on the car, you can't sell it. Nope, not to anyone but the depositor. However, if the car remains unsecured, you sell it to the first buyer who gets to you. This should arouse his concern enough to send you a deposit if he's really serious.

The amount and length of the deposit's effectiveness varies. Deposits are usually between $100 and $500, and the time constraint can be as long as you can stand. Be good to your buyer, though. Tell him to make the effective date for a comfortably lengthy period, and that you'll send him a receipt to cover his interests. You can accept a personal check because it will have long enough to clear. Be accommodating. That's all there is to it.

But you do need a "Plan B." Should he not come through for some reason, be absolutely certain that you continue to take names and numbers of interested callers. You are definitely into the homestretch at this point in the sale, but more than one horse has stumbled on the last link.

When other people call, it feels good to tell them

the car is sold. But also tell them that if the deal falls through, you'll be happy to contact them. They may inquire as to the agreed selling price, in which case, I usually tell them. This will trim subsequent negotiations to a bare minimum in case you want to recontact these people. I would gauge their enthusiasm before I volunteered the sales price, however.

Once you get your deposit, be sure to cement the trust you've labored to get by sending your buyer a receipt. It needn't be filled to capacity with legalese, but certainly equipped with the essentials: The date of receipt, the amount of money, the people, the merchandise, the termination date. These five ingredients should suffice. (There is a sample receipt in the Appendix.)

If your buyer experiences difficulty with the closing that is beyond his control, you'll have to do some soul-searching in respect to holding the deposit. Should he request to delay the closing, you may want to issue him an extension of time, which is no real problem unless you have people lined up to come look at the car. However, if he cannot close at all, that's another matter . . . and a tricky one at that. Only once in my life have I not refunded a deposit, and that was due to a ludicrous situation. (Then again, five years ago, a crook in Tennessee kept a deposit of mine for no good reason and I still gleefully entertain thoughts of dropping a rabid wolverine down his chimney.) You will not make friends by keeping someone's deposit, but this may not be the friendship you want. Keeping a deposit is really a last resort, even though you never indicate this to the buyer. The deposit's purpose, as discussed, is defeated if you leave gaping loopholes in the agreement.

From the moment your buyer commits to the purchase, you two are more or less on the same side of the fence. Or at least meeting at the same fence in a coexistence of sorts, aimed at closing the deal. The "other side" mentality is nearly eliminated, and it's time to work together. I only say "nearly" eliminated due to the small percentage of times when someone complains that you didn't tell him about the scratch on the tow hook or the bent page in the owners manual. These people respond well to a little ego massaging on being so observant, but mostly you are in for a meeting of the minds that accomplishes the original intention—selling your car.

I've yet to discuss that little detail concerning payment method. You'll need to attend to this before the guy shows up trying to pay you in pesos. Most buyers will ask how you'd like to be paid. The preferred method is by cashier's check. To further enhance the two parties similitude, tell him for his protection it would be best if the cashier's check was made out to both of you, requiring both signatures for it to be deposited or cashed.

Some people will say that they'd rather write you a personal check. Well, it seems there is a small percentage of bad-check writers that gives every check writer a bad name, so you'll have to discourage the personal check openly. It doesn't matter if the car is only $500, that's grand larceny if the check is no good. And just try to make it worth some lawyer's time to track this schmuck down and get your car back or make the check good. No sir. Even the sweetie at K-Mart gets you to sign a "Waiver of Citizenship" should that check you wrote for Lectra-Shave be returned. If K-Mart can't afford the risk, you can't either.

You can be ultra-frank (but polite) and tell the customer that as much as you'd like to help him, you just can't take a personal check. If he persists on the grounds of convenience, just put enough deterrents in the check-writing option to make it *less* trouble to get the cashier's check. First, tell him you'll need a letter of credit on bank letterhead signed by his banker. The check will have to be received during banking hours, so you can call to verify and hold funds. Lastly, you don't release the title until the check clears. This way, there is no way the "convenience" of check writing can logically outweigh that of the cashier's check.

You may have a buyer who wants to bring cash. This just scares me twist-legged, but it sort of matters how much cash we're talking about. You be your own judge as to how much is too much to be carrying around. I still contend that a cashier's check made out to both parties is *the* way to do it legally, safely and securely.

Your last-minute checklist before the buyer's arrival is to make sure of the following.

1. Your car looks as good as it can look.

2. You've topped up gas, water, oil and any other fluid levels. You've checked air in tires, *plus* spare.

3. You've cleared with the buyer his exact payment balance and exact arrival times (in the proper time zone).

4. Your paperwork is ready to be transferred.

5. Any spares that you promised are ready to go.

After reviewing these items, you are ready to meet your buyer, and at long last close the deal.

Chapter 3

The inspection

"What's that horrible noise that sounds like marbles in a blender?"

"Oh, that. Oh, yes, I can hear it now . . . that's just some pebbles my child put in the hubcap. Do you have children?"

Hmmm. Ever been to a used car lot and heard mechanical or human noises like this? The human (sort of) response was technically a "minimalization/diversion." No, plenty of car salespeople can't pronounce it, but they know what it is. This book is written primarily for individuals selling to other individuals, so you probably won't be dealing with people who sell cars every day for a living and are therefore familiar with these techniques. But that's not to say that you'll be greeted by the Pope, either.

You are making the effort to inspect a car that is one thing: what it was represented to be. But beware of your own imagination. The mind's eye has a tendency to see what you'd *like* it to see, as opposed to what it was or wasn't said to be. And it's the "wasn't said" that worries me. Continuing the dialogue above, did you ask about the transmission and differential? If you did, and he said it was okay and it is determined to be very un-okay, then you must adjust the situation as needed, all the while taking no stock in what else he says. But if you didn't ask, then you must take a small portion of the blame.

So, remember, your interview sets a precedent for what is to be expected of only those areas covered in the interview. But now you're at the car and you can press your evaluation a step further.

In making your evaluation, be sure to make written or mental notes of any problems. If you aren't going to have a mechanic do an additional inspection, you'll need to know approximate costs for repairs. For those using a mechanic, be sure to discuss your findings in detail to get his professional opinion.

Look at the car. Every angle. High and low. Kneel down at the front or rear where your sight line follows the length of the car and look for uniformity. Any waves? Difference in paint texture or slight color variation at body breaks? Should you notice any irregularities, this car has probably had some bodywork. Tap with your fingernail in the suspected area and surrounding areas. Does the tone change from a hard, empty sound to a dullish, thick sound? If so, that's body filler. If a magnet won't stick to the would-be steel area, that's a sure indiction of filler, too. Look very, very closely and you may see sanding scratches in the affected area. At this point, don't ask *if* it's been repaired, ask how severe the damage was.

Look around the entire lower portion of the car for evidence of rust. Feel inside any body cavities. The wheelwells and trunk, too. Under the spare. Anywhere moisture can contact the car and be held in place. Rust appears as scales, bubbles or rough edges, and it can attack almost anywhere, but especially at seams, low areas and around trim. If the car has been driven in salt and has a few years on it, it probably has some rust. If the rust has affected structural areas, leave the car alone unless you really know what you're getting into or just want a parts car.

Inspect the area around all trim, rubber and chrome for any signs of body-color paint in places it wasn't painted from the factory. Commonly referred to as "overspray," this merely indicates the car has been repainted to some extent. Whether or not you find any filler in the car, ask why it was repainted. If you find evidence of other colors it could mean one of two things: The car has had a color change or, if the other color shows up on just one body panel, that panel was replaced with a used part. Find out why. Remember, not if, but *why*.

Look again at the chrome, especially near the tail pipe where exhaust toxins cause corrosion of chromium-plated surfaces. New chrome or rechroming old parts isn't cheap.

Inspect all glass and lenses.

As you're walking around the car, push each corner of the car with a force generous enough to spring it. If it bounces back and stops, the shocks are good. If it bounces more than once, you need shocks. Visually inspect the shocks for leakage to confirm their condition. While in the suspension region, check the tires for wear, quality and matching. Good tires are rightfully expensive, as bad tires adversely affect the car's roadability.

Open the doors, trunk and hood. Look at the weatherstripping. Is it dry or torn? Are there stains on the carpet or in the trunk from water seepage? Check for headliner stains, especially around the sunroof or rear windows. During the road test remember to listen for wind leaks or whistles. If air can get through, water probably can as well. Weatherstripping is far more expensive than you'd ever guess by looking at it.

Now shut the doors firmly but without slamming. Do they feel solid and tight, or do they drag a bit? The driver's door is usually the one to suffer, since it's used more frequently.

The same holds true for the driver's seat. Look at it carefully. Scan the entire interior. Behind seats, around carpet edges, door panels, dash top, everywhere. If you replace just a piece of upholstery or part of the carpet, will the rest of the interior match properly, or is it faded?

If it's a convertible, how is the underside of the top? Outside? Check for tears, specifically in the area where the top frame collapses and could pinch the top. Is the rear plastic window clear? Light "fogging" can be removed but heavy distortion stays. Check top frame for rust and ease of operation. (On British cars, "ease of operation" is a relative term.) Lift the mats and feel for any dampness. Glance under the dash for stray wires or any nonfactory splicing.

Under the hood, check for general cleanliness of the engine. An owner fastidious enough to keep an engine clean (as opposed to one who had it steam cleaned prior to your arrival) has probably been good about maintenance. Be complimentary and you'll find out more. On a not-too-clean engine, do you see oil seepage all over the block or on the underside of the hood? If it's clean on top but looks oily at a place where parts meet and below, you've probably got a leaky gasket at that junction. A valve cover gasket is not expensive to replace; if it's the head gasket, expect a sizeable expense.

Unscrew the oil filler cap and inspect it for moisture; do the same with the oil dipstick. (Of course, note the oil level.) Should you see water beads or a grayish "milky" color, you've got a probable internal problem. Now check the radiator cap for oil. If oil is present, the verdict is the same: expensive.

Look at all the belts and hoses for wear. No, this isn't a big expense, but it's a major pain if any one of these breaks on the drive home. Look at the underside of the belts for fraying and check the tightness. Any more than 3/4 inch of play is too much. As for the hoses, give them a good squeeze to see if they are too mushy or wood-hard. Either condition indicates replacement time.

Again, under the hood, look for loose wiring of any sort and make an inquiry to the owner. Check the battery terminals and holding box for corrosion.

Walk to the back of the car and have the owner start the car. Look for smoke on the initial start-up, a little of which isn't too frightening if the car has been sitting for awhile. Have him operate the brake, taillights and blinkers. As the car warms, check the oil pressure gauge (hopefully so-equipped) and make note of the reading. At the front of the car, check the parking lights, head lights, blinkers and auxiliary lights.

Then back under the hood—to just listen. If you hear knocking, try to determine the source and inquire. A knocking deep within the engine is bad news. Should you hear any hissing noises, it's probably a vacuum line that has cracked, which is inexpensive to replace but problematical to the driveability. Listen to the idle for evenness. You don't want to hear a loping, uneven sound.

Now, again as you're walking to the back of the car, check the oil pressure and water temperature. After a few minutes of running, the oil pressure reading will drop a bit (as the oil viscosity lessens) and the water temperature will raise to within the operating range but hopefully no higher. Once at the rear, have the owner rev the motor a time or two, and watch for smoke. Bluish smoke indicates oil burning; whitish smoke is usually an improper mixture in the carburetors. Take a dollar bill and hold it right at the tail pipe during idle. The bill should blow freely away, as you'd expect, but if it ever "pops" back toward the tail pipe, you've likely got a valve problem. Visually inspect the exhaust system and listen for any raspy-sounding leaks or overall loudness. A complete exhaust system replacement can be quite expensive, and a leaky one is potentially lethal, so be sure you check thoroughly.

Now have the owner go from Park to Reverse to Drive (automatic transmission) and back with his foot on the brake. Any loud clank here can be from U-joint problems to loose bands to other transmission maladies. On a power-steering-equipped car, get him to move the wheel lock-to-lock and listen for any whining or squeaky sound. A slight squeak at each turning extreme is fairly normal, any more should be checked.

Ask the owner to move the car away from where it has been idling for these few minutes and look for fluid drippage of any sort. Brownish to black oily spots came from the engine; dab a small amount on your finger and smell it to see if there is a gasoline smell, which indicates at best an overrich carburetion setting or at worst a problem with the piston rings. If it's the milky color described earlier, that's water. Not good. A reddish fluid is either transmission or power steering fluid, so there's a leak somewhere that needs attention.

Your turn to take the wheel. Depress the brake or hold it firmly for fifteen to thirty seconds. If it gradually depresses more, you've got a system leak. Now pump the brake pedal. If it rises on each of two to three pumps, then you have air in the system. No problem to get the air out, but how did it get in there? Ask.

Now operate every switch and control to make certain they all function properly. *Everything*. Remember to check air conditioning, heat, defrost and so on, regardless of season.

To test clutch slippage on a manual transmission car, set the handbrake, depress the clutch, engage first and begin to release the clutch as you would to drive off. The car should stall. If it doesn't and the brake is holding, you've got clutch slippage. You can also check the clutch by accelerating briskly in third gear while doing the road test. Should the engine overrev in relation to the car's speed, then the clutch slips. Check the synchronizers for smooth shifting up or down without grinding. Lots of cars (particularly Italian ones) have slow second gear synchros, but it should get smoother once fully warmed up.

While driving, keep an eye on the temperature and pressure levels. Should the oil pressure drop considerably during the test drive (below manufacturer's specifications) or once idling again, you've got problems. And they may not be confined to the car. If the car had really exceptional oil pressure at start-up and then dipped below average after warming, the owner may have used a super-thick cure-all oil for a low-pressure engine—a cheap, mask-over of a major expense. A compression test will probably belie the early reading. Look for smoke in the rearview mirror. If it should smoke on acceleration, that's probably piston ring wear. Smoke on deceleration is usually valve guide wear.

Being very careful that you're clear of traffic on a straight road, release the steering wheel (but keep your hands very nearby) and apply the brakes. Should the car veer, there is an alignment problem or the brakes need adjustment, or both. If there is a vibration in a certain speed range only, then the tires need balancing. A vibration felt in the seat is usually rear wheels, vibration in the steering wheel is usually front wheels.

Keep taking mental notes of the overall driveability. How does the engine feel? Does it hesitate when pulling from stops, or does it respond properly throughout the rpm range. If you've driven other cars of this make and model, how does your impression of *this* car fare? Were the brakes as tight, the steering as precise, or the handling as compliant? It is the comparative evaluation that is so helpful in the road test because it gives you a yardstick with which to measure.

On a manual transmission, go through all the gears, checking for any crunching now that the car is warm. Any better? With an automatic, check the up-shifts for smoothness during acceleration *after* slowing to about 10 mph or so. This should have down-shifted the transmission to first gear, then push it through its course of high-low-high shifting. There should be smooth, positive shifting with no slips or jerking. On either transmission, be certain to check reverse gear, which is commonly overlooked. Keep an ear open for any unusual noises and try to pinpoint their location. Pay attention to all the gauges during your drive as well as making sure the odometer works.

Once you've completed the test drive (or driven to your mechanic), let the car idle for a few minutes to see if any fluids begin to leak. Now, shut the car off for a minute or two and open the hood. Scan for fumes, hissing, steam, smoke or anything out of the ordinary.

Then restart the engine, again checking gauges for good readings. The car should restart easily and return to a normal idle. Turn the car off again. Take a good hard overall look at the car while it cools to see if you notice anything new.

Once the tail pipe is cool enough to touch, check to see what type and color deposits are just inside the rim. Light gray to tan are just fine. A black, powdery substance is usually a carburetor maladjustment. A black, oily deposit is trouble. Ask the owner how much oil the car consumes. It's preferable to do this after your test drive because it's an easy, revealing check that can just as easily have been wiped clean prior to your arrival.

I know this inspection will take some time and effort, but wouldn't it be a pain if you had gone through this entire process only to get stung on a bad car? You don't need that. Additional certainty would be ensured by having a mechanic inspect the car after your assessment. Ask plenty of questions and compare notes.

The inspection has nothing to do with trusting the owner, because he may not have known about all of what you discover. If perchance an innocently overlooked but needy repair does surface and it doesn't turn you away from the car, be diplomatic. You must impart your discovery into a last-minute negotiation. Tell the owner that, naturally, your offer had been based on finding a car that was just as represented save for this small, but significant oversight. Would he be willing to reduce his price by that of the repair? If he says no or is reluctant, modify your terms with that old stand-by of splitting the difference, which is utterly fair and usually acceptable. If he accepts either proposal, be thankful to him and the presence of your "buffer" money.

Whether doing your inspection solo or with the aid of a mechanic, it can only enhance the likelihood of making a good purchase.

Chapter 4

The closing

Ah, yes. The closing. The final treaty and heap big exchange. Conditional discrepancies and any last-minute negotiations are closed. (Sound the buzzer.) The process itself is really quite simple and short, but as usual there can be variations dependent upon the titleholder/lienholder, as previously discussed. However, there are virtually no variations in the essence of documents it takes to transfer ownership. If you've contacted the title bureau in your state (whether buying or selling), you'll know what is necessary to complete the transaction: Proof of Chain of Ownership, and a Bill of Sale.

I can almost hear you asking what a Proof of Chain of Ownership is, so I'll tell you it is most often a title, but there are situations where no title exists, so this all-inclusive term is used. The car may be registered in a state where no title law was in effect at the time of the car's manufacture, or some other legitimate reason. But, of course, you've already settled this long ago, haven't you? And since you have, we can press on to the Bill of Sale.

The Bill of Sale is more or less a receipt. It will complement the other documents and be supporting evidence of the sale, which is why it should be notarized or at least witnessed with another signature. It also details the specifics of the sale by telling when, who, where, what and how much. (See the sample Bill of Sale in the Appendix.)

At the closing, if you don't use my Bill of Sale, simply make sure these questions are answered. Don't just accept any old "Received $500 for car. Signed _____." This may serve your immediate purposes, but if a question should ever arise, you won't have the answers, *especially* if there's not a title, either. Without proper documentation, you are asking for problems from the Department of Motor Vehicles, and these people are the absolute best at annointing one's soup with flies. In fact, I believe it's requisite for the job.

Now we come to how this ties in with the all-important payment that is exchanged for these documents. Mainly, you must "match" all paperwork, or make all the pertinent information the SAME, that is: Signatures, Amounts, Merchandise, Exactly.

Signatures must match how the preprinted documents are made out. The name on the title, the Bill of Sale and the check must all match exactly. If there's a "Jr." following a name, don't think it doesn't matter if you leave it off. Yes, it most definitely does, because *with* "Jr." and *without* "Jr." are two different people.

Amounts must be matched where applicable. I once accepted a cashier's check for $1,100, which was just dandy except that it was supposed to be for $11,100. Thank goodness for an honest buyer who had dealt with an equally honest but new bank teller. The numerical and written amount must also match exactly. In case of a discrepancy, the official ruling is in favor of the written amount, so be careful.

Merchandise where described must be to the letter, or number as the case may be. If it says "Triumph," don't just put "TR." Check the serial numbers at least twice. Some manufacturers use as many as twenty digits or letters. Miss one number and you may be quickly consumed in red tape. The same applies to year model.

Exact matching on these very important documents is easy to overlook but difficult to overcome. Keep a clear head and pay close attention for the few minutes it takes.

Before and after the actual paperwork, there is a bit of pomp that I happen to like. A handshake. Sure, you'll probably shake hands when you greet each other, but I'm talking about a handshake to cement the terms. Either the buyer or seller can say aloud what the conditions and terms are to be, and then shake hands on the deal. You may think this is old-fashioned, out-moded, passe, whatever, but I think it's a personal, effective means of conveying agreement. After the signing, a handshake distances the litigation stiffness and allows for a return to free-breathing.

For the closing process, keep the acronym SAME in mind at all times, and be sure to read the documents carefully. The buyer and seller need to keep watchful eyes on key ingredients. Is the title clear and readily transferrable? If not, is the banker aware of where the transferred title is to be sent? Make sure the Bill of Sale reflects any changes or additions that you have made verbally. Again, if any parts or agreed payment of repairs or *anything* on the buying or selling end was verbalized as part of the agreement, write it into the Bill of Sale. Taking the word of a mere acquaintance is a noble and honorable gesture, but in reality it is an open invitation for risky relations.

You needn't feel odd about including additional items on the Bill of Sale because it is actually a part of the sale, and leaving it out is leaving it to chance. Ask any attorney about the leverage of a written over a verbal contract. Aw, skip the leverage part, ask about the sheer *rightness* of the clear, written word. (You may get a dissertation for a reply, but don't say you weren't warned.)

The next two documents—the title and the cashier's check—have the legal side covered and should be signed at the same time. The title need only be signed by the seller, whereas the check is endorsed by the buyer(s) in the "Pay to" or "Payee" blank. The seller will endorse the check upon deposit.

All this paperwork is absolutely worthless until it's signed. It goes from a few grams of worthlessness to gaining enormous legal weight when signed. The title—with one signature—has totally transformed ownership rights to the car. The check could be torn up and laughed at until it's fully endorsed, whereby it becomes real, live, spendable money. Prior to signing, the Bill of Sale is a useless bunch of words . . . then it becomes a legal document denoting this valuable transaction. The signatures make the deal, in a figurative and literal way. So if you have an ounce of hesitancy at the point of signing, take a breather and think about it if you must, because you want to be sure. Very sure. You can't grab your marbles and go home; this one is for keeps.

In another very real way, the closing has become the single definite point into which all your prior energies have been funneled. The buyer has seen his research come to fruition. The seller's efforts have been equally rewarded. And each has just moved to another position in the automotive experience.

Buying or selling a car by long distance is a fabric woven of many threads. Your initial interest, determination, awareness, absorption, response and ability to communicate freely are all stitched tightly together at the closing. And without being overly analogous, the process takes drive, if you will. Drive carefully to arrive safely and honestly at your destination. It has been my pleasure to help get you there.

Appendix

Receipt of Deposit

I, _____1_____, have received from _____2_____

a deposit of $ _____3_____ to secure the purchase of

_____4_____   _____#_____

until _____5_____.

_____6_____   _____8_____
                                        Date

_____7_____

1. Your name typed or printed.
2. Buyer's name.
3. Amount received.
4. Year, make, model, serial number.
5. Termination date.
6. Your signature.
7. Witness' signature.
8. Date signed.

Bill of Sale
(A)

I, _____(B)_____, do hereby transfer my rightful and

legal ownership of one _____(C)_____. (# __(D)__)

to _____(E)_____, for the agreed sum of

_____(F)_____ which was paid in full on the

date of this transaction, _____(G)_____.

This vehicle is free from all liens and encumbrances

except that in favor of: _____(H)_____.

_____   _____
        Name   Address

_____   _____
       Amount   Phone

_____   _____
        Seller   Buyer

                                  _____
                                   (Notary Public)

A. You must entitle the document.
B. The seller's name (as it appears on other documents).

C. Year, make, model of auto.

D. Serial number (double-check for accuracy).

E. The buyer's name (as it appears on the check).

F. The written dollar amount followed by the numerical amount in parentheses.

G. The date of the signing.

H. If there is any money owed on the vehicle, the information goes here; if not, put N/A (not applicable).

Odometer Statement

(Optional to Bill of Sale)

_____
Date

_____ (#_____)
Year   Make   Model   Serial

The above described vehicle with mileage indicated hereon of _____ is:

____ correct to the best of my knowledge.

____ incorrect due to inoperability or odometer replacement and the estimated corrected mileage is _____.

____ in excess of 100,000 miles plus the mileage indicated.

_____   _____
(Seller)   (Witness)

Inspection outline

How to use the inspection outline:

Read through the entire outline. Familiarize your-self with what is applicable in your specific case. On the initial interview, ask generally about the major headings first, and then work through to specifics. With any answer that sends up a red flag, continue your line of questioning until the information is satis-factory. Don't spend time cluttering your memory. Take notes.

I. **Cosmetics**
    A. Exterior
        1. Paint and body
           a. Rusted
           b. Wrecked
           c. Repainted
           d. Dings, chips, scratches, dents
           e. Faded, mismatched
           f. Overall paint finish
        2. Chrome and trim pieces
           a. Pitted, rusted
           b. Rechroming
           c. Rubber trim
           d. Aluminum, stainless, black chrome
           e. Rubber trim, weatherstripping
           f. Lights and lenses
        3. Glass
           a. Cracked, broken, chipped
           b. Frosted
         4. Convertible top
           a. Type material
           b. Rear window
           c. Tears, rips, seams, seals

        5. Overall cosmetics
        6. Work needed
- B. Interior
  1. Seats
     a. Material
     b. Rips, tears
  2. Dash top and face
     a. Cracks
     b. Distorted, faded
  3. Knobs and gauges
  4. Carpet
  5. Door and kick panels
  6. Headliner (underside of top)
  7. Overall appearance
  8. Work needed

II. Mechanical

- A. Mileage
  1. Original
  2. Over 100,000
  3. Odometer replaced
  4. Verifiable
- B. Maintenance history
- C. Engine
- D. Transmission (clutch)
- E. Rear end, differential, axle
- F. Brakes
- G. Steering
- H. Suspension
- I. Tires, wheels
- J. Electricals
- K. Gauges and accessories
- L. Overall mechanical
- M. Work needed

III. **Other**

    A. Options, accessories
        1. Original
        2. Aftermarket
    B. Ownership
        1. Owned how long
           a. Problems during ownership
           b. Problems now other than mentioned
        2. Any liens
           a. Lienholder's name
           b. Approximate payoff amount
        3. Previous owner(s)
           a. How many
           b. Names, numbers
    C. Miscellaneous
        1. Receipts for work
        2. Owners manuals
        3. Spares

Appraisers

There aren't many automobile appraisers who advertise out of their local market, mostly due to travel expenses. The first three on this list are unquestionably the most visible advertisers and have been in business many years. They also happen to be located conveniently in each major US region.

Robert DeMars
989 40th Street
North Oakland, CA 94608
415/655-7123

Cy Kay
1160 Waukegan Road
Glenview, IL 60025
312/724-3100

James T. Sandoro
24 Myrtle Avenue
Buffalo, NY 14204
716/855-1931

Ted Handler
2028 Cotner Avenue
Los Angeles, CA 90025
213/474-8831 or
213/479-1197

James Martin
43 Bowdoin Street
Newton Highland, MA 02161
617/332-9069, AM only

Steve Cram
1080 Eddy Street, #607
San Francisco, CA 94109
415/567-1087 or
415/456-1942

Title bureaus

These states will provide information about car titles by telephone:

State	Department	State	Department
Alabama	205/271-3250	Nevada	702/885-5505
Alaska	907/269-5551	New Hamp.	603/271-3111
Arizona	602/255-7425	New Jersey	609/588-3649
Arkansas	501/371-2824		or 292-4121
California	916/732-7243	New Mexico	505/827-7581
Connecticut	203/566-4410	New York	518/449-3419
Delaware	302/736-4468	N. Carolina	919/733-3025
DC	202/727-6680	N. Dakota	701/224-2725
Florida	904/488-3881	Ohio	614/752-7671
Georgia	404/656-4100	Oklahoma	405/521-3217
Hawaii	808/942-3745		or 521-3221
Illinois	217/782-9787	Oregon	503/371-2200
Indiana	317/232-2861	Penn.	717/787-3130
Iowa	515/281-5277	S. Dakota	605/773-3541
Kansas	913/296-3621	Tennessee	615/741-2477
Kentucky	502/564-2737	Texas	512/465-7611
Louisiana	504/925-6146	Utah	801/533-5311
Maine	207/289-3071	Vermont	802/828-2000
Maryland	301/787-2970	Virginia	804/257-0523
Mass.	617/727-8500	Washington	206/753-6946
Michigan	517/322-1624	W. Virginia	304/348-3910
Minnesota	612/296-2977	Wisconsin	608/266-1466
Missouri	314/751-4509		or 266-3666
Montana	406/846-1424		
Nebraska	402/471-3910		
	or 471-3913		

These states do not provide title information by phone:

Idaho—Idaho Transportation Department, Titles and Registration, PO Box 34, Boise, ID 83731. Fee of $2 per vehicle should accompany letter. In-state dealers can call 208/334-4666.

Mississippi—State Tax Commission, Title Division, PO Box 1383, Jackson, MS 39205. Minimum fee of $4 on current title or verification of title. Fee should be included with letter.

Rhode Island—Submit an application form, along with a $5 fee. To get an application call 401/277-3100.

South Carolina—Dept. of Highways and Public Transportation, PO Box 1498, Columbia, SC 29216-0024. Fee of $2 should accompany letter.

Wyoming—Dept. of Revenue, 122 W. 25th Street, Cheyenne, WY 82002-0110. Fee of $2 should accompany letter.

Magazines

Here is an annotated list of publications you may consider for placing an ad.

Auto Trader's Old Car Book
PO Box 9003
Clearwater, FL 33518
813/531-8061
    Compilation of national ads with photos from local auto trader sources. Very extensive coverage but cars are not alphabetized. Very reasonable rates.

AutoWeek
1400 Woodbridge
Detroit, MI 48207
1-800-722-7798
    One of the few large, weekly magazines on automobiles. Excellent classified section devoted primarily to sports, imports and collectibles.

Automobile Magazine
Auto Sphere Dept.
755 2nd Avenue
New York, NY 10017
    The upstart broad-market car magazine aimed at *Road & Track* readers. Has done co-op individual car ads with *DuPont Registry*, but is otherwise slim in classifieds. Monthly.

Car Collector
8601 Dunwoody Place
Suite 144
Atlanta, GA 30338
    Covers mostly postwar US cars. Has a rather slim, but well-targeted classified section.

Car Exchange
3816 Industry Boulevard
Lakeland, FL 33803
    Excellent variety in automobiles, but more slanted toward American nostalgic or muscle cars. Reasonable rates.

DuPont Registry
6200 Courney Campbell Causeway
Suite 340
Tampa, FL 33607
1-800-233-1731
1-800-262-2886 in FL.

Ultra-slick, all advertising for high-end luxury, sports, exotics. Expectedly expensive. Lengthy word allowance plus full color. Monthly.

Hemmings Motor News
Route 9 West
PO Box 380
Bennington, VT 05201

The grandaddy of the special-interest automotive marketplace. Very reasonable rates. If it's related to special-interest cars, it's in *Hemmings*. Monthly.

Old Cars & Parts

Just what you would expect from the name. Mostly cars of US origin. Reasonable rates. Monthly.

Old Cars Weekly
Iola, WI 54990

Tremendous circulation to mostly American car buffs. Very reasonable rates.

Road & Track
1499 Monrovia Avenue
Newport Beach, CA 92663

Old faithful. Excellent monthly of primarily performance cars in text and classifieds. Fair rates for market covered.

Robb Report
One Acton Place
Acton, MA 01720

Not a car magazine per se, but certainly first-class "Premium Motorcars for Sale" section that is essentially the forerunner of the style used in *DuPont Registry*. Rather expensive, but so are the cars.

Sports Car Illustrated
AutoShowcase
PO Box 5241
Station-E
Atlanta, GA 30307

Another *Robb*-type layout in color, but in a full-fledged car magazine that is faithful to its name.

Price guides

NADA (National Auto Dealers Association) Official
Used Car Guide
8400 Westpark Drive
McLean, VA 22102-9985

This book is widely used by dealers because of its clarity in denoting additions or deductions for options, mileage, and condition. Quite explicit and complete, has regional editions plus additional books on older cars.

Black Book
PO Box 758
Gainesville, GA 30503
404/532-4111

A long-time favorite of bankers for determining loan values of late-model vehicles. Also used by dealers. Generally lower pricing than the NADA.

CPI (Cars of Particular Interest)
PO Box 11409
Baltimore, MD 21239

Essentially a *retail* price guide to postwar collectible or special-interest cars. Gives low, high and average prices by year, make, model. Updated quarterly.

Old Car Price Guide
Iola, WI 54945

Just what the name implies, but has recently expanded coverage up to 1979 model year. Mostly concentrated on US-built cars, but includes a good smattering of foreign makes. Gives a numerical rating (I–IV) for condition.

Edmunds Price Guides
515 Hempstead Turnpike
West Hempstead, NY 11552

Friend to the consumer, *Edmunds* spells out the material associated with dealer cost, mark-up, option prices, plus specifications on individual cars. *Edmunds* publishes numerous consumer-oriented guides.

Auto Price Almanac
Pace Publications
1020 North Broadway
Milwaukee, WI 53202

Another consumer guide that emphasizes the "actual" prices of the cars, options, dealer charges, mark-up and so on.

Price Guide to Collector Cars
House of Collectibles
201 East 50th Street
New York, NY 10022

Excellent coverage, quite extensive. Thousands of car prices (literally), A–Z, domestic and foreign.